PRAYERS from the PARKING LOT

Prayers from the Parking Lot

50 short reflections for moms on the go

MARY CARVER

Revell

a division of Baker Publishing Group
Grand Rapids, Michigan

© 2022 by Mary Carver

Published by Revell
a division of Baker Publishing Group
PO Box 6287, Grand Rapids, MI 49516-6287
www.revellbooks.com

Printed in the United States of America

Library of Congress Cataloging-in-Publication Data
Names: Carver, Mary (Writer), translator.
Title: Prayers from the parking lot : 50 short reflections for moms on the go
    / Mary Carver.
Description: Grand Rapids, MI : Revell, a division of Baker Publishing
    Group, [2022]
Identifiers: LCCN 2021058172 | ISBN 9780800740818 (paperback) | ISBN
    9781493436422 (ebook)
Subjects: LCSH: Mothers—Religious life. | Mothers—Prayers and devotions.
Classification: LCC BV4529.18 .C385 2022 | DDC 248.8/431—dc23/
    eng/20220110
LC record available at https://lccn.loc.gov/2021058172

The author is represented by the literary agency of The Blythe Daniel Agency, Inc.

Baker Publishing Group publications use paper produced from sustainable forestry practices and post-consumer waste whenever possible.

22   23   24   25   26   27   28   7   6   5   4   3   2   1

To Annalyn and Adrienne

Contents

DON'T MAKE ME PULL OVER!

RUNNING OUT OF GAS

SHIFTING GEARS AND CHANGING LANES

Introduction

Hey there, mama.

How are you? If you're anything like me, you're busy, probably to the point of feeling exhausted and overwhelmed. You're worried, possibly even anxious about those kids of yours. You're certainly not looking for another thing to put on your to-do list (or to feel guilty about never crossing off that list). Maybe you're even hiding from the kids and the list right this minute, desperate for even a moment to yourself while you wait on piano lessons or speech therapy or karate class to finish.

You are not alone. Well, you're alone in your car (or your hiding place of choice), but you're not alone in the exhaustion or the overwhelm. I hear you, and I get you.

All of this—everything that holds us moms in the driver's seat for just one more minute before hauling the groceries inside, combined with the eleventy billion things the world throws at us every single day—is why I'm more grateful than ever for the gift of prayer. I'm grateful for a God who welcomes us with open arms every time and any time we turn to Him.

But more than that, I'm grateful He wants the real version of us, not some cleaned-up, got-it-together, fancy-talking version we think we need to be.

No, ma'am. He wants us just as we are, in whatever state (or parking lot) we're in right now. He's ready to listen when we're worried, when we're scared, when we're tired, when we're bursting with pride. He wants to pull us close whether we're dressed to the nines or we're wearing the same ponytail and leggings for the third day in a row. God loves us in every season and stage of mothering, and He is waiting for us to turn to Him in the midst of our good days, our hard days, our everyday. Messy bun, messy van, and all.

Take a minute to breathe when you can, and let the short prayers of this book guide you to God.

Whether you're hiding in the bathroom, folding another load of laundry, or pulling into soccer practice at the last minute, take a few moments for yourself. Take the burdens and the blessings, the worries and the wonders of motherhood, and bring them to God. He's right there waiting for you, even in the parking lot!

Love from a fellow mom on the go,

Mary

Buckle Up!

Today a man introduced himself to me at my daughter's basketball game.

Him: "Hi, I'm Nick, Millie's dad."

My reply: "Hi, I'm Mary, Adrienne's dad."

In case anyone's wondering how the last year and a half has affected my social skills.

❧ 1 ❧

WHEN YOU NEED TO ASK FOR DIRECTIONS

If any of you lacks wisdom, you should ask God, who gives generously to all without finding fault, and it will be given to you.

James 1:5 NIV

When our kids are small, answers to (or at least opinions on) our most pressing parenting questions can be found around every corner. The trick at that stage is discerning which answers are actually right for us and avoiding the pitfalls of inaccurate info or unhelpful advice. But as our kids grow up, guidance seems to dry up. One day we wake up with suddenly hormonal humans, these newly complex kids—and we realize we have no idea how to help them navigate shifts in social status, deal with disappointment, and handle heartbreak or even homework. While tips abound for mastering sleep training and potty training, how-to guides for older kids are few and far between. Thankfully, God's wisdom applies to every age and stage, and when we ask Him, He will always direct our path toward knowledge and understanding.

None of us are given a handbook or an instruction manual when we become mothers. Yet, from the day our kids enter our homes to the day they move out for the last time, we are bombarded with questions and confusion. Mentors, mom groups, and magazine articles might answer some of our questions for the moment, but only the Lord can offer the lasting, life-giving wisdom we truly need. Leaning on Him will give us direction as well as peace of mind that we're doing the very best for the ones in our care.

Lord, I need You. Just when I thought I had a few things figured out, everything changed and now I'm lost again. I don't know how to parent a child this age. I don't know how to teach him and protect him and make sure he knows that he's loved. What do I do? Please guide me. Point me to the wisdom You've laid out in Scripture; show me what to read and what to do with Your words. I know You are working behind the scenes to make everything come together for our good and Your glory. And I want to be a part of that. I want to work with You, and I want to do the right thing for my kid. Please, Lord, give me wisdom. Give me clarity and confidence in what I hear from You. Show me what to do. Thank You. Amen.

2

WHEN WORRY ISN'T WORKING

> Don't worry about anything; instead, pray about
> everything. Tell God what you need, and thank him
> for all he has done. Then you will experience God's
> peace, which exceeds anything we can understand.
> His peace will guard your hearts and minds as you
> live in Christ Jesus.
>
> Philippians 4:6–7

When my kids were young (and, I'll confess, even when they weren't so young), I devoured every sob story and cautionary tale about the things that can go wrong in a child's life. Every rare disease, every random injury—I wanted to know about them all so I could be prepared and maybe even prevent them from happening to my family if I tried hard enough. My husband shook his head and wondered out loud if perhaps I was creating my own stress. But I was insistent: the only thing that could prevent catastrophe was my continuous cataloging of possible problems.

Eventually, I realized that no matter how long my list of fears was, it would never be exhaustive—though it would be exhausting. And even if I did manage to cover every single thing that could harm my children, that was no guarantee I wouldn't someday find my own story on that list. I couldn't protect my kids with worry and pure strength of will, but I know the One who can protect them with His power and love.

As I began praying more for my kids and trusting that God would answer those prayers, my heart finally felt at peace. Choosing to place our kids and every concern we have about them in God's hands will put our hearts and minds at ease more than any list of worries or doomsday preparation ever could.

God, forgive me for believing I'm in control and my family's well-being depends on me. Help me remember that You love my kids more than I can imagine and that You can hold them safely while also taking all the burdens I try to carry. Help me rely on You and not myself, remembering all the ways You've provided in the past and finding peace in You and not in a list of worries I've made. I want to stop worrying, Lord. Help me let go and trust You. Amen.

3

WHEN GROWING KIDS REQUIRE GROWING COURAGE

Haven't I commanded you: be strong and courageous?
Do not be afraid or discouraged, for the LORD your God
is with you wherever you go.

Joshua 1:9 CSB

Every time I took my daughter to the park, the big slide caused both of us great anxiety. She worried that she would fall off and break open like Humpty Dumpty; I worried that she would never be brave enough to do big things. Both of us were overreacting to the slide situation, and neither of us was being strong or courageous. This happened over and over, year after year, until one day—she did it. She climbed to the top and, instead of turning around and squeezing past the kids in line behind her, she whizzed down the slide!

What seemed like only a day later, the two of us began to face much bigger and scarier situations. Field trips I couldn't chaperone, overnight church retreats, ziplining and roller skating, her own email account, friends I'd never met—all of a sudden the big slide didn't seem so scary. But just like I assured her that God would be with her and keep her safe on that slide, God assures me of that when I fear for her safety now. Both my girl and I can be strong and courageous, knowing that God is with her wherever she goes.

God, I'm scared. Honestly, I am constantly afraid for all the ways this world can hurt my children. But I know You tell me not to fear; You tell me to be brave and strong. It's no coincidence that I tell my children the same thing, even when I'm feeling terrified myself. I don't want them giving in to fear, and I know You don't want that for me either. So, Lord, I'm asking today that You help me trust You for my children's safety. Fill me with strength and courage. Remind me that You are with me—and with them—wherever we go. Amen.

WHEN YOU NEED TO BE GENTLE

Always be humble and gentle. Be patient with each other, making allowance for each other's faults because of your love.

Ephesians 4:2

*B*eing patient is hard enough, but being gentle? That feels impossible some days! Whether it's a late afternoon email from my boss with another urgent task, a child forgetting her important assignment (or lunchbox or shin guards or permission slip) at home, or inconsiderate drivers slowing us down when we are on a schedule and already behind, life gives us plenty of opportunities to lose our patience and our humanity.

But God wouldn't ask us to be gentle and understanding if He didn't also help us live out those fruits of the Spirit. Scripture tells us that all things are possible with God—even this. So let's go to God when we feel the pressure of expectations and deadlines and mistakes and irritations. Let's look to the Lord when we'd really rather roll our eyes and toss out sarcastic or resentful barbs. Let's ask Him to help us be humble, patient, and gentle.

Lord, help me. Help me remember that I'm not the only person with a schedule or a to-do list or feelings or concerns. Help me see others as brothers and sisters, not as obstacles or inconveniences. Especially when it comes to my children, God, please keep my heart soft and my words gentle as I treat them the way I want to be treated, the way You want me to treat them. Thank You for leading me to live in a loving way, even when it feels so hard. Thank You for helping me be patient and kind. Amen.

5

WHEN YOU WONDER, "IS THIS NORMAL?"

Your own ears will hear him.
Right behind you a voice will say,
"This is the way you should go,"
whether to the right or to the left.

Isaiah 30:21

Nothing can make a mom freeze in uncertainty like three little words: *Is this normal?* So many doubts and anxieties are wrapped up and ramped up with that question. We wonder if it's normal for our kids to cry uncontrollably when we drop them off at school—or we wonder if it's normal for them to climb the steps of the school bus without a single look back. (For what it's worth, I had one of each of those on their first days of kindergarten!) Truly, feeling unsure about what's typical, what's healthy, what's dangerous, what's temporary, or what's life-altering for our kids can push a mom over the edge.

But what if "normal" isn't really a thing? What if we're holding our kids and ourselves up to the wrong standards when we get sucked into the comparison game through Google searches, parenting forums, and late-night texts to our friends? Each one of us and each one of our kids has been wonderfully created in God's perfect image. And that is the only answer we need when we begin searching for "normal."

Let the Lord calm your anxious heart as you remember that your children are His masterpieces, designed on purpose and with a purpose. Let us lean on Him as we learn to love every unique thing about them.

God, is this normal? Is what my child doing normal? Is how I feel normal? What does "normal" even mean? Oh Lord, please help me. Help me remember that You have uniquely and wonderfully created my child (and me). Bring me peace and empower me to trust You with everything we're going through. Forgive me for freaking out, and help me breathe deep as I remember to rely on You, no matter how unusual or unexpected things get or how seemingly "normal" they really are. Thank You. Amen.

6

WHEN IT'S JUST A PHASE
(AND WHEN IT ISN'T)

You know what I am going to say
    even before I say it, LORD.
You go before me and follow me.
    You place your hand of blessing on my head.
Such knowledge is too wonderful for me,
    too great for me to understand! . . .
You saw me before I was born.
    Every day of my life was recorded in your book.
Every moment was laid out
    before a single day had passed.

Psalm 139:4–6, 16

Of all the unhelpful comments parents receive, "It's just a phase!" might be one of my least favorites. First of all, when you're living through a difficult season, it feels unending even though you know it won't last forever. Well-intentioned or not, a reminder that our feelings aren't accurate can come across as dismissive or insensitive.

Second, how can you know if what your kids are struggling with right now is a temporary challenge? How can anyone know? We can't. When we're in the moment, parenting in the trenches, taking each day as it comes and making the best decisions we can with the information we have, we don't know if the hard thing keeping us up at night will ever go away. We don't know if our kids will be OK or if they will deal with this for the rest of their lives. We don't know. But God does.

God knows exactly what's around the bend and even farther down the road, and He'll be with us and with them every step of the way.

Dear God, I wish I could ask all my questions and demand answers today. Will my daughter ever make good friends? Will my son struggle with math forever? How much does it matter if they don't make the team or get cast in the musical? Is she always going to struggle with anxiety or addiction? Will he ever return to the truths we've taught him all these years? I wish I could know now, but since I can't, I'm trusting You. I believe that You have a plan for my kids, and I believe it's a good one. Thank You, Lord, for giving them a future and for giving me (and them!) hope. Amen.

7

WHEN YOU'RE IN A SCHOOL ZONE

Get wisdom—
how much better it is than gold!
And get understanding—
it is preferable to silver.

Proverbs 16:16 CSB

I have so many boxes of flash cards in my house. I find them in the dining room, in the guest room, and occasionally even in the car. I'm always optimistic, thinking that we'll use them to practice math facts or sight words or how to tell time on a clock face (something my kids love to remind me they cannot do). But you know what we never do at my house? Use flash cards. (See also the stack of "fun" workbooks I've bought for my kids to use every summer since they started school.)

Don't get me wrong. I'm actually tremendously grateful because both my girls love school. But that doesn't mean we haven't had struggles (hello, middle school math, I'm talking about you!), and I don't assume school will be a piece of cake over the next several years either. Various parts of school—whether it's a specific subject, different learning styles, connecting with teachers, or something else entirely—will always present challenges for our kids (and for us). But even as we work through the good and bad of school, we can support our kids most by praying that they desire and seek knowledge and a heart of wisdom as they grow.

God, thank You for the opportunities You've given my kids to learn. Thank You for their school and their teachers. Please give them a hunger for learning, Lord. Give them a desire not just for information but for understanding, not just for knowledge but for wisdom. Show them how what they're learning affects their daily lives; show them how their education fits into the "real world." Give them strength and perseverance when school is difficult, and give them new challenges and new problems to solve as they master skills. Amen.

8

WHEN YOU'RE AFRAID YOU AREN'T GOOD ENOUGH

For it is God who is working in you both to will and to work according to his good purpose.

Philippians 2:13 CSB

How many times do you collapse on the couch after your kids finally go to bed, depleted and discouraged, convinced you've failed yet again? Do you wonder, as scenes from the day flash before your tired eyes, if your kids would be better off with a different mom? Maybe someone more gentle or creative or adventurous or energetic? Maybe a Pinterest mom or an Instagram mom or that patient, put-together mom you see in the church lobby as you and your crew stumble in, mismatched and irritable and running late again?

I've been there, questioning myself and my ability to parent my kids. Many times. But I've also heard the reassuring whisper (or exasperated shout) of a friend reminding me that no, my kids would not be better off with a different mom. Those words of truth echo Scripture rather than my own doubts and fears, and they bring me back to what I know at my core: God doesn't randomly give us kids for no reason and leave us to flounder on our own. No, instead He's specifically working in us and through us according to His good purpose for our kids and for us.

God, it's easy to believe my kids would be better off with a different mom—or, if I'm honest, to wonder if I'd be better off with different kids. Forgive me for doubting Your plan, Lord! Forgive me for questioning Your design, both for families in general and for my family in particular. And forgive me for the ways I fall short again and again. Please help me live out Your purpose for my life and support my kids as they do the same. Show me how You've created me to be the exact mom they need. Amen.

WHEN YOUR PLATE IS TOO FULL

No one can serve two masters, for either he will hate the
one and love the other, or he will be devoted to the one
and despise the other. You cannot serve God and money.

Matthew 6:24 ESV

I've never met a mom who didn't feel pulled in ten different directions at any given moment. Whether or not we receive a paycheck for the work we do, every mom wears multiple hats and manages numerous responsibilities. And no matter what shape our work takes, most moms feel torn at some point when deciding which item on our to-do list should take precedence over the others. We're all juggling too many balls, and attempting to keep them all in the air feels like a circus act. It's something that's true for all of us, but so is the good news of Jesus.

The Son of God didn't make life more complicated when He came; He made it so much simpler. He boiled down all the rules and responsibilities of life to this: love God and love others. When we focus on God and give our relationship with Him first priority, it allows Him to put us back together and enables us to put everything else in its rightful place instead of being pulled in even more directions.

God, I have a confession. Sometimes when I think about how I should spend more time with You or make You my top priority, I feel so guilty. And then I feel frustrated. How can I add one more thing to my list? I try to do everything for everyone, and instead I feel like I'm letting everyone down. Will serving You first really make things better? Will You show me? Teach me how to make You my top priority, Lord. Reorder my to-do list and my life and my heart. I will follow You. Amen.

⚘ 10 ⚘

WHEN PINTEREST
MAKES YOU PANIC

I am sure of this, that he who started a good work in you
will carry it on to completion until the day of Christ Jesus.

Philippians 1:6 CSB

Sometimes I panic when I see Pinterest posts with the "ulti-
mate list" of what kids should know by age ten or twelve or
eighteen. I remember how I forgot to teach my oldest daughter to cut up her own food until she was nine years old, and I
think about how many chores and recipes and skincare tips
I still haven't taught her. I think about the day when my kids
will leave home, and I wonder how they could possibly take
care of themselves when just last month I realized that I've
never taught either of them how to answer a landline or ad-
dress a letter or make spaghetti.

Thankfully, God doesn't leave us alone to panic *or* to parent. I remember who taught me to change a flat tire, shave my

bikini line, and make pumpkin bread. It wasn't my mom. And that's OK! I value the lessons I learned from my mom, and I'm still learning from her today. But as moms we aren't expected to teach our kids every single thing they need to know. We can ask God to give our kids other teachers, other resources, and a desire to keep learning how to be the amazing people He created them to be.

God, thank You for filling in the gaps where I fall short. Thank You for TikTok tutorials and cool aunts and teachers who take extra time to go over the basics I forgot about. Please guide me as I make the most of the time I have with my kids, and give me wisdom to share with them. Show me ways I can teach them while we go about our days—practical things, like how making a double batch of dinner will save time later, and spiritual things, like how listening to worship music can keep us calm in the car. And remind me that You will finish the good work You started in them, which I've been privileged to be a part of. Amen.

God, forgive me for believing

I'M IN CONTROL AND

MY FAMILY'S WELL-BEING

DEPENDS ON ME.

Caught in a Traffic Jam

9 p.m. on a Friday. Sitting outside the middle school in my SUV, wearing yoga pants and eating Girl Scout cookies while I jam to 80s music. Pretty sure I unlocked a mom level tonight.

11

WHEN WORDS HURT

God blesses you when people mock you and persecute you
and lie about you and say all sorts of evil things against
you because you are my followers.

Matthew 5:11

One of the most incredible things about the internet is
the way it allows anyone to say anything. No longer do
we need a publisher, a platform, or permission to share our
innermost thoughts, feelings, and opinions with the masses.
Of course, while we are allowed to say whatever we want, so
is everyone else. If someone wants to say hurtful or hateful
things to or about us—or, worse, to or about our kids—they
can. And at some point someone probably will. What then?

Often our first instinct is to strike back or launch a defense
campaign on behalf of ourselves or our loved ones. Though
we say "Sticks and stones may break my bones, but words will
never hurt me," the truth is that being mocked, criticized, or
lied about can cause deep pain. It's wise to take the necessary

steps for keeping ourselves and our kids safe online, unfriending or unfollowing those who cut us down and reporting those who cross the line into bullying. But we can also find great comfort in Jesus, remembering that He has experienced this same kind of slander and abuse. He quite literally feels our pain. And when we act with integrity by loving others even when it means we need to draw boundaries, God will bless us with abundantly more than anything those hurtful words took from us.

Jesus, thank You for enduring persecution for my sake. I know You understand how I feel right now. What my child is (or I am) going through is so painful. It's not fair that someone can say such hurtful things! But I know You will fight our battles for us. We can trust Your promises, and experiencing Your love and protection in such a way will bless us more than we can imagine. Keep me steady, Lord. Fill me with Your love and give me strength when enemies attack. Amen.

⚜ 12 ⚜

WHEN IT'S HARD TO TRUST GOD

Trust in the LORD with all your heart,
and do not lean on your own understanding.

Proverbs 3:5 ESV

Sometimes the world just doesn't make sense. When your daughter practices and trains for hours every day but still doesn't make the team. When your son digs deep for the courage to start a conversation or make a connection but still can't make any friends. When your kids are bullied or injured or frustrated or left out. These things don't make sense. And when it comes to lost jobs or deadly viruses or racial injustice or a cancer diagnosis? We can feel devastated and disoriented, and wrestling with it all can leave us wondering, "Where is God? What's He doing? What is He calling *us* to do?"

When our world is especially harsh and our kids are affected, we can begin thinking that we're alone in helping them handle it. It might feel like explaining hard things is all up to us. Like navigating new challenges or fighting the same ones that keep coming up is a burden we bear alone. But no matter what our circumstances—or our kids' circumstances—look and feel like, we can trust that God is still good, that He is still in control, that He is still with us and will never leave us. We can trust that He loves our kids even more than we do. We can trust Him.

Dear God, why is this happening? Are You still with me? With my kids? It's so hard to see them hurting so badly, and I just want to fix it. Or at least I want to understand it. I know You see the whole picture, and I believe You are working all things out for our good. Will You show me something good in this situation, even if that something is simply Your presence with us? Help me trust You with all my heart and with those who have my heart. Thank You, God. Amen.

⚘ 13 ⚘

WHEN YOUR KIDS ARE BEING BULLIED

Be strong and courageous; don't be terrified or afraid of them. For the LORD your God is the one who will go with you; he will not leave you or abandon you.

Deuteronomy 31:6 CSB

When our children are hurting, moms hurt too. And when someone else is intentionally causing them pain—well, sometimes moms want to cause pain in return! (Just ask me how I felt the moment I heard a fourth-grader call my kindergartener ugly names at the bus stop.) But just like we teach our kids that seeking revenge will only make a situation worse, unleashing our Mama Bear instincts on whoever dares hurt our babies can be the last thing our families need.

I'm not saying we shouldn't protect our children. In fact, do inform the appropriate authorities if your child is in danger or being bullied. I absolutely believe our job is to keep our kids safe whenever we can, but we are also tasked with teaching them how to courageously and compassionately navigate a dangerous world. And as they grow, we can't go everywhere they go. Sometimes they have to face their foes on their own. When that time comes, we must trust God to go with our kids, to never leave or abandon them. And then we must teach our kids to trust God too. That way, no matter what—or who—they face, they know they're never alone.

God, please protect my child. I know I can't roll her up in bubble wrap or always keep her within arm's reach, much as I'd like to. But I also know how dangerous this world can be. And right now, she's hurting and she's scared. Please give her (and me!) confidence that You are with her and will never leave her. Give her strength and courage, but don't let her heart become hard. Give her wisdom to know when to stand firm and when to seek help. Keep her safe. Amen.

❧ 14 ❧

WHEN YOU NEED GOD TO PROVIDE

Consider the ravens: They don't sow or reap; they don't
have a storeroom or a barn; yet God feeds them. Aren't
you worth much more than the birds?

Luke 12:24 CSB

Is anything weightier than the responsibility of providing
for our families? Our number one job as parents is to take
care of our children, and that can be so difficult at times! We
may face unexpected expenses that wipe out any cushion
we had—or that leave us wondering how we'll pay for them
at all. Braces, allergy shots, school supplies, and shoes for
feet that never stop growing are just a few things that seem
to come up when we least expect it—and often when we are
least prepared. Even harder, we sometimes find ourselves in
a longer season of struggling to feed and clothe our family,
desperate to figure out how to cover even the basics.

Whether you're worried about paying for college in a few
years or you're unsure if you can keep the lights on this week,

God is ready and waiting to hear your concern and to help you. Take your troubles to Him, and He will listen and provide. That doesn't mean you'll win the lottery tomorrow; no Bible verse makes that promise! But He will give you what you need for the moment, just like He gave the Israelites the manna they needed for each day.

God, I need Your help. I love my kids so much and want to give them every single thing they need, but it's so hard. Will You help me? I know You're more powerful than bills and budgets, and I know You see solutions where I see only problems. Please open my eyes to ways I can take care of my family. Please make a way for them to have what they need. Thank You today for what You're going to do tomorrow. Thank You for loving us. Amen.

✺ 15 ✺

WHEN THEY NEED A DETOUR AROUND HARMFUL MEDIA

Guard your heart above all else,
for it determines the course of your life.

Proverbs 4:23

*P*arenting can take your breath away, but not always in a good way. Finding a steamy romance novel under your young child's pillow or a violent video game stashed in the basement can feel like a punch in the gut. Feeling betrayed, disappointed, scared, angry—these emotions may threaten to overpower your conviction that a calm response is needed. *How could they do this? Why would they do this? Does it matter? Am I overreacting? Is this my fault?*

All those questions and more are likely to race through your mind until your head is spinning. But the number one question you're probably asking yourself is, *What do I say here to teach them to make a better choice?* Resources from parenting experts abound, and practical tips can certainly be found (and should be shared), but the simplest answer can be found in Scripture. When teaching our kids to turn away from the harmful images and words so easily accessible in media, we can begin with the same thing God has told us: *Guard your heart more than anything else, because what's in your heart affects your whole life.*

> *God, this is so hard to talk about—even with You, but definitely with my kids! It's awkward and uncomfortable for all of us, but I know it's important. Please guide me to the resources that will help me protect and teach my kids as they learn to navigate a world full of words and pictures that can hurt them. Guard my heart and theirs, and show us how to focus on only those things that honor You. Thank You, Lord, for Your wisdom and Your grace. Amen.*

❧ 16 ❧

WHEN TEMPTATION SNEAKS IN

The temptations in your life are no different from what others experience. And God is faithful. He will not allow the temptation to be more than you can stand. When you are tempted, he will show you a way out so that you can endure.

1 Corinthians 10:13

A few days ago I found an opened and nearly emptied bag of mini marshmallows in my pantry. "Did you do this?" I asked my kids, even though the answer was obvious. I'd left them alone in that part of the house, and when they foraged for something to munch on, they easily found the "forbidden fruit." (Never mind that the marshmallow bag was found mere inches from actual, healthier fruit . . .) My first instinct was to lecture them about why eating too much sugar is dangerous and how being sneaky is the same as lying. But unlike other times when I've found evidence of similar crimes, I paused.

My kids weren't off the hook for their sneaky snack. They know ripping into a bag of what are essentially sugar cubes is not OK. But the incident gave us an opportunity to talk about temptation and how God promises to always give us a way out—whether we're tempted to stuff our faces with sugar or to do something even more harmful or dangerous. We talked about how we can recognize temptation and pause to ask ourselves if we have another, better option in that moment. And I reminded my kids (and myself) that when we find ourselves being tempted—whether by marshmallows or by more serious issues like cheating on a test, vaping or smoking, or spending time on harmful websites—we can ask God to help us make the better choice.

God, I am so grateful You give us everything we need, including a way out whenever we're tempted to go our own way instead of following You. Thank You for giving me the strength to resist shouting at my kids and shaming them when they make mistakes, and thank You for forgiving me when I make the same mistakes they do! Please show me how to teach my kids to turn to You for help in avoiding sin and for grace when they don't. Thank You, God. Amen.

⚘ 17 ⚘

WHEN IT'S TIME TO SPEAK UP

Speak up for those who cannot speak for
themselves;
ensure justice for those being crushed.
Yes, speak up for the poor and helpless,
and see that they get justice.

Proverbs 31:8–9

Anyone who's ever broken a cookie in half for two siblings
to share knows that kids are highly concerned with justice. They seem to walk around this world on high alert for
any hint of bias or discrimination, always looking out for any
perceived slight, any excuse to holler "It's not fair!" Of course,
they're usually focused on what's fair for them and how they
are being mistreated. But because of this deep desire they
have for equality, they're often receptive to learning about
how they can seek justice for others as well.

Teaching kids about people who are helpless and hurting
can be difficult. We don't want to steal their innocence or

burst their bubble of believing that the world is good and safe. I've cried every single time my kids have had to learn about another injustice, from homelessness to childhood cancer to terrorism. But by allowing them to see how other people live and the challenges they face, we can open them up to opportunities for great compassion and generosity. And if we ourselves make a point of speaking up when we see injustice in the world, we teach our kids to use their "it's not fair" radar for the good of others.

God, thank You for the tender heart You've given my child. Please give me wisdom as I teach her about the world we live in and about all the ways we can help others. Give us opportunities to use our voices, our resources, and our influence to work toward justice for all. Show my child how other kids are living with much larger problems than the small half of the cookie or a sibling who always gets to hold the remote or kick the ball first—and give her the desire to help. Teach my kids and me to speak up for those who cannot speak for themselves. Amen.

⚜ 18 ⚜

WHEN YOU NEED HELP FOR BROKEN HEARTS

The LORD is near the brokenhearted;
he saves those crushed in spirit.

Psalm 34:18 CSB

The afternoon I had to tell my daughter that her favorite uncle had died in a motorcycle accident is branded into my brain. I can't imagine I'll ever forget that devastating moment. It was the first time, but unfortunately not the last time, I watched my child's heart break. Since then I've seen both my kids face shattering realities that crushed them, and while I am their soft place to land, ready with hugs and acceptance and assurances that eventually it will get better, I can't fix everything.

Whether it's the loss of a family member, the end of a friendship, a disappointment on the field or stage, or even a hard realization about human nature, our kids are going to experience heartbreak. We can count on it—even though we don't want to. When heartbreak happens, moms often feel helpless as we watch our kids suffer. We know that nothing we say or do can ease their pain in that moment. But no matter what kind of tragedy has struck, no matter what nightmare has come true, we can take solace and strength in remembering—and in teaching our kids to remember—that God is always with us. He specifically promises to be near the brokenhearted. And that's something to count on with gratitude and gladness.

God, I'm so glad You're here with us. Thank You for loving us so much and never leaving our side, even when it feels like the whole world is against us. Right now, my baby is hurting, and I don't know how to make it better. Will You make Your presence known to him today? Wrap him in Your arms and heal him from the pain he's feeling. Remind him that he is loved and that You have good plans for him. And please show me how to help him too. Thank You, God. Amen.

☙ 19 ❧

WHEN YOU NEED TO PUT THE BRAKES ON SCREEN TIME

Finally brothers and sisters, whatever is true, whatever is honorable, whatever is just, whatever is pure, whatever is lovely, whatever is commendable—if there is any moral excellence and if there is anything praiseworthy—dwell on these things.

Philippians 4:8 CSB

After height and weight, screen time often feels like the thing that gets measured most in our lives as parents. Figuring out how much screen time is appropriate and then enforcing that standard feel like equally difficult tasks (and both chores make me long for the days when this wasn't even an issue . . . until I remember how thankful I am for other modern conveniences!). And then, just as soon as we make a decision and commit to it, our kids or our circumstances change, forcing us to pivot once more.

But as our kids grow, we need to not only monitor their time using screens and media but also begin teaching them how to make healthy choices for themselves. Of course, that's when it gets really tricky! Parents can find countless resources and recommendations for healthy screen-time habits. But sometimes those guidelines seem to contradict each other or don't apply to our family's specific needs, and we can end up more confused and unsure than ever. And let's not forget our own temptation to spend more time staring at a screen than into our kids' eyes and the example that's setting for them. Turning to Scripture, God's enduring Word, is a good place to start and a good way to remind us all that we should focus on whatever is true, honorable, lovely, and pure—both on-screen and off.

God, is it just me or does parenting get more complicated every day? I need Your help here, Lord. Please guide me as I talk to my kids about how much time they spend on screens and what they do while they're plugged in. Help me instill in them a value for truth and beauty and everything that honors You. Help me set healthy boundaries and a good example by putting down my own devices and experiencing this world You've created in real life. Thank You for Your Word and Your timeless wisdom. Amen.

20

WHEN YOUR CHILDREN HARM THEMSELVES

He heals the brokenhearted
and bandages their wounds.

Psalm 147:3 CSB

Something about becoming a mom turns even the most gentle spirits into fierce defenders, ready to take on anyone who dares hurt their babies. But what's a mom to do when her baby is the one causing their own pain? Oh, what a unique and piercing heartbreak this is! To learn that our kids are making choices and engaging in behaviors that are certain to hurt them deeply can shove us into a spiral of desperation as we try to figure out how this started, why it's happening, how long it's been going on, and—most importantly—how we can make it better.

One of the worst parts of realizing that our kids are choosing to harm themselves is that we may not be able to make it better. We can confront them or take them to counseling. We can assign consequences and offer a shoulder to cry on. We can do all the right things, but unlike the days when we could kiss boo-boos better, we can no longer heal all their pain. What we *can* do, though, is place them in God's hands through prayer, trusting that He will do what we cannot and guide both us and our kids on this journey.

God, I need You. My child needs You. Will You please make it better? She's hurting, and I don't know how to reach her, how to help her. I wish a Band-Aid or special song or popsicle would do the trick like it did when she was little, but nothing I do seems to make a difference. I'm afraid she's going to hurt herself or someone else beyond repair, and I don't know how to stop that from happening. Please help us, God. Give us guidance and strength for the path ahead of us. Amen.

God, help me trust You

WITH ALL MY HEART

AND WITH THOSE

WHO HAVE MY HEART.

Don't Make Me Pull Over!

I sprayed deodorant in my hair this morning thinking it was dry shampoo. If anyone's wondering how my day is going.

☙ 21 ❧

WHEN GRATITUDE IS HARD
BUT HELPFUL

Be thankful in all circumstances, for this is God's will for
you who belong to Christ Jesus.

1 Thessalonians 5:18

Feeling thankful is easy on the good days, isn't it? When
the kids listen and follow directions; when they help a
friend, win the game, or bring up their grades; when they
actually eat the dinner you fixed them without complaint—
gratitude comes naturally. (Or at least I assume it does on
that last one. I'm not sure I've cooked a single meal that made
every person in my house happy.) But when life is more complicated or challenging, we struggle to find gratitude. It's in
those times, though, that we need it more than ever.

Taking time to thank God for our children—and for our job
as their mother—can reset our hearts and help us see them
with eyes of gratitude and love, even when they do or say

things that we're not exactly thankful for! Doing this points our hearts and minds back to God and often gives us resilience, peace, and joy, even when they refuse to try the dinner we lovingly prepared or pick yet another fight with their siblings. True thankfulness will keep us focused on the most important things and will help us forget the rest (or at least put it into perspective).

God, thank You for giving me these kids. Thank You for making me their mom. Thank You for their spirit and spunk, and thank You for every glimpse of sweetness I get. In the hard moments, please help me remember what a blessing they are, and keep me mindful of the amazing gift they are. When I'm tempted to grumble or to focus on the challenges of parenting, please keep me mindful of how grateful I am. Help me to see the mundane minutiae of our life together through Your eyes, to recognize laundry and dishes and appointments and arguments as reminders that these children filling up my home and heart and life and lap are precious and so loved. Thank You, Lord, for my children. Amen.

❖ 22 ❖

WHEN THEY WON'T JUST GET ALONG

Do not say, "I'll do to them as they have done to me;
I'll pay them back for what they did."

Proverbs 24:29 NIV

ut she started it!" What parent hasn't heard those words? No matter how close and cooperative siblings might normally be, at some point they'll disagree. And more than likely they'll fight and fuss, ratcheting up the friction until someone blows and someone else pushes back. From there, it's *he said this* and *she did that* and *it's not fair*, until pretty soon words might be spoken or actions taken that have a more lasting effect than anyone intended.

As moms who love our kids and desire not only peace and quiet in our homes but also healthy, affectionate, supportive relationships between our children, we can easily slip into guilt mode when they fight. Or even if we don't blame ourselves, we can quickly become despondent, believing that if our kids can't get along now, they'll never be friends when they're older. But before we take either of those paths, let's try one more thing. Let's ask the Lord for help. Before the next argument begins (or right now while they carry on in the back seat), let's go to God and ask Him to meet us right where we are and work in all our hearts.

God, thank You for my children. I know You created them with their exact personalities and gave them to me exactly when You did for a reason. But Lord, those personalities and ages are all the excuse they need for antagonizing and arguing with each other! Please give me patience. Give me strength to hold my tongue and not escalate the tension in our home. Give me wisdom and show me how to negotiate their disagreements, and help us all work together to find solutions and a renewed dedication to loving one another well. Be with us, Lord. Amen.

23

WHEN THEY FORGET THEY'RE MADE IN GOD'S IMAGE

The LORD doesn't see things the way you see them. People judge by outward appearance, but the LORD looks at the heart.

1 Samuel 16:7

Both of my daughters are tall. And even though I distinctly remember how awkward I felt about my own height when I was in my tween and teen years, I was surprised recently when one of them shared how she hopes she doesn't grow anymore. Shortly after that conversation, I overheard one of her friends remark on my daughter's height, and I remembered how cruel the world can be to those of us who don't fit the mold of what's expected or accepted.

As my little girl asked me why her friend would say that and confessed how it made her feel, I looked her in the eyes and assured her that every part of her was still perfectly designed by God. I reminded her that God is creative and makes each one of us different, and I told her again that she is beautiful. We also talked about how what we see with our eyes doesn't necessarily tell us the whole story about a person. And then I heard an undeniable whisper telling me the same is also true of me.

I suspect I'll have many more conversations like this with both my girls; you'll likely have them with your kids too. When that happens, let's embrace those opportunities to speak words of kindness and truth to our kids—and to ourselves.

God, thank You for being the most creative Creator, for making each one of us different and calling each one of us "good." Please remind me, just as I remind my child, that You made me like this for a reason and that You love me exactly the way I am. Help me be a good example of appreciating the way You created me, and show me opportunities to speak words of affirmation and love and truth over my kids. Show us the beauty in all of Your creation, including the beauty in ourselves. Amen.

❦ 24 ❦

WHEN SOCIAL MEDIA PRESENTS NEW CHALLENGES

Let no corrupting talk come out of your mouths, but only
such as is good for building up, as fits the occasion, that
it may give grace to those who hear.

Ephesians 4:29 ESV

Has such an enormous temptation for "corrupting talk" ever existed as the internet? Perhaps. But we cannot deny the way scrolling through the endless thoughts and opinions of others—or staring down a blinking cursor and hundreds of potential readers—can stoke the flames of our harshest criticism, unhealthiest fears, and tendency to strike first. We set aside our compassion and common sense for the mere moments it takes to leave a scathing comment, share an unconfirmed rumor, or simply blast as many as we can with the words that seem so necessary in the moment.

As our kids begin dipping their toes into online communication, we coach them to think twice about the words and images they share—and we'd be wise to remind ourselves of that too. When we log on and participate in on-screen communities, let's remember to do what we teach our children: Treat everyone the way you'd like to be treated. Say (or write) only words that are true, helpful, inspiring, necessary, and kind. And use every avenue of communication to build up, never to tear down.

Dear Lord, please forgive me for the times I've allowed corrupt, harmful talk to come out of my mouth. Holding my tongue (or, when it comes to social media, my fingers!) can be so hard, but I know what You require. Show me how to take every opportunity to encourage others, and protect me from the temptation to hurt anyone. Open my eyes to the ways I've used my words to harm, and point me to the ways I can help others instead. Lord, make me an instrument of Your love and Your peace—and a good example to my kids. Amen.

≈ 25 ≈

WHEN YOU REDEFINE HOSPITALITY

Above all, love each other deeply, because love covers
over a multitude of sins. Offer hospitality to one another
without grumbling.

1 Peter 4:8–9 NIV

I often ask my children if they would speak "that way" (the
way they just snapped at me) to their teachers, coaches, or
grandparents. I ask if they'd talk "like that" (the way they just
taunted their sister) to their best friend or even a classmate.
Of course, their answer is always no.

It never fails, though . . . as soon as I begin this line of correction, I always hear the same questions echoed back to me.
Not from my kids (they wouldn't dare!) but by the still, small
voice of the One who whispers truth in my heart even when
I'd rather play pretend. *Would you talk to your coworkers or Bible
study leader or next-door neighbor that way? Are you loving your*

family as deeply as you love the people who don't live in your house? My answer is often the same sometimes defiant, sometimes remorseful "no" I get from my kids.

What the Bible calls "hospitality" could also be called friendliness, warmth, kindness, generosity, or courtesy. And that's how I want to treat everyone, both inside and outside my house.

God, thank You for the Bible and the wisdom it contains about how we should treat one another. Forgive me for the times I am unkind or harsh to my family; please help me treat them hospitably. I want everyone in my house to feel safe and welcome, not in a fake-nice way but in an authentically accepting and loving way. Please show us how, Lord. Thank You for the work I know You're going to do in our hearts. Amen.

☙ 26 ❧

WHEN THEY NEED TO BE
REMINDED THAT KINDNESS COUNTS

Get rid of all bitterness, rage and anger, brawling and
slander, along with every form of malice. Be kind and
compassionate to one another, forgiving each other, just
as in Christ God forgave you.

Ephesians 4:31–32 NIV

My child would *never* do that!" Who among us hasn't had
that thought? We hear about kids picking on someone
who's a little bit different or starting rumors about someone
who used to be their friend. We see a child trip or shove or
snub their peer, or we read a memo from school informing
parents of a dangerous trend among students. And every time,
our first reaction is to think, "*My* child would never do such
a thing."

I thought that myself, until the day I chatted with another
mom and discovered that my daughter had been mean to

her daughter—so mean that this mom hoped the girls would be placed in different classes the next year! The girls later became the best of friends, but my eyes were opened. While I still counsel my kids about what to do if they're being bullied, now I also tell them stories or give them books about people being kind to others. I point out opportunities for us to care for people, and then we act on those opportunities together. I teach them how God tells us to be kind and compassionate to one another. If we want it to be true that our kids would never hurt others, we can't leave it up to chance or just assume that we've taught them to know better.

God, I want to believe that my child would never hurt anyone. But I also know that my sweet, obedient kid is human and therefore susceptible to temptation, peer pressure, and, let's not forget, hormones! Please show me every opportunity for teaching my kids to be kind, Lord. Show me where I can be kinder and model the compassion You command us to offer others. Help me forgive when my kid messes up, but don't let me neglect my responsibility to teach them what I want them to know and to do. Thank You for showing us what kindness looks like. Amen.

27

WHEN YOU NEED TO GIVE AND RECEIVE FORGIVENESS

If we confess our sins, he is faithful and just and will forgive us our sins and purify us from all unrighteousness.

1 John 1:9 NIV

You hate me now, don't you?" I was gutted when my daughter muttered those words. While I should have been shocked that she could possibly believe such a thing, I understood how she'd come to this upsetting conclusion. Behaving like an irritable teenager myself, I'd been refusing to speak to her after spewing bitter criticism and disappointment at her earlier that day. I told myself my silence was to protect her from more harmful words, but honestly it was also to punish her. I certainly didn't hate her, but I knew I hadn't acted in love either.

In my desperation to teach her a lesson, I'd gone too far. I'd abandoned mercy for the sake of justice, becoming an immovable force blocking our way to forgiveness and healing. My daughter, who had made a mistake just as I've made hundreds of mistakes, believed she'd gone too far and saw no pathway to redemption—all because I let my anger rule the day.

Have you been there? Lost your temper, tossed out words you regret, and become a roadblock instead of a compass your kids can follow to growth and forgiveness? Thankfully, God offers forgiveness more freely than we do, and He promises to wipe away our sins and to help us move forward together.

God, please forgive me. Forgive me for getting so angry with my kids and for making them feel anything less than loved. Forgive me for holding them to an unrealistic standard and for prioritizing rules over relationship. Forgive me for the ways I've disobeyed You, and show me the way of righteousness. Thank You for Your mercy, Lord, and please help me offer that same mercy to my children. Give me a soft heart full of compassion and grace as I guide them toward growth and healing. Amen.

28

WHEN ANXIETY STRIKES

You keep him in perfect peace
whose mind is stayed on you,
because he trusts in you.

Isaiah 26:3 ESV

Anxiety is much more common than many of us realize, and it's a growing problem among children and adults. And while we instinctively anticipate there will be many childhood challenges, from scraped knees and ear infections to eating disorders or even addiction, anxiety is something that often takes us by surprise and leaves us unsure how to help our struggling kids. Whether our children battle everyday fears and worries or a chemical imbalance that requires medical treatment, we can feel as overwhelmed as they do in these situations. How do we know if anxiety is the cause of their behavior? How serious is it? How do we help them?

When our kids have anxiety, it's easy to feel scared as we wonder where it came from and if it will ever go away. But while anxiety is a serious situation and we should absolutely seek professional help when needed, God doesn't want us living in fear. We can find peace in trusting Him with our kids, even as we seek peace for them as well.

Dear God, I'm so worried about my child. He's struggling with anxiety, and not knowing how to help him or when it will get better is making me feel anxious too! Please help us. I trust You with his mind, body, and soul; I do. Protect him and heal him, and while You're at it, Lord . . . will You help me too? Give me peace and confidence that You are holding him in Your hand, that You will never leave him or me. Thank You. Amen.

✺ 29 ✺

WHEN OUR WORDS SET THE WRONG EXAMPLE

A gentle answer turns away anger,
but a harsh word stirs up wrath.
The tongue of the wise makes knowledge attractive,
but the mouth of fools blurts out foolishness.

Proverbs 15:1–2 CSB

The day I heard my youngest daughter shout a swear word, I was shocked. She'd heard it used in the television show we were watching, and she not only used it correctly but also didn't understand at first why I was so disturbed. After all, if the characters could say it, why couldn't she? That incident upset me but was quickly remedied. The day I heard my oldest daughter speak to my husband with the kind of disrespect she'd heard me express toward him was even more upsetting—and revealed a problem much harder to solve.

Whether it's profanity, gossip, criticism (of ourselves or others), or even a disrespectful or unkind tone—our kids hear it all. They are constantly watching us and listening to us, learning how to treat others from our example. And hearing our words come out of their mouths can be the harshest reflection of our hearts that we never asked for! Kids will never simply "do as I say, not as I do"; that's not how they're wired. It's hard to change the way we speak, which really begins with the way we think. But it's worth the effort to use our words wisely—and God will help us do it.

Dear God, please forgive me for the ugly ways I've spoken to or around my kids. I forget that they're always listening, always soaking it up, and now I have regrets. Please show them the mercy of helping them forget the times I've been a bad example, and help me be different now. Help me speak words of kindness, forgiveness, grace, and love. Help me use my words and my influence with my kids wisely. Thank You, God, for helping me to speak love and life. Amen.

✥ 30 ✥

WHEN WE WANT TO GRUMBLE AND COMPLAIN

Do everything without grumbling and arguing.

Philippians 2:14 CSB

When I tell my kids to fold their laundry or empty the dishwasher, their response often leaves much to be desired. Their body language says it all: *The audacity! How dare you impose on us with this outrageous demand!* My response to them is equally dramatic, as my eyes widen and my nostrils flare. Though I don't say it out loud, I almost always think to myself, *How dare I? How dare you! Do you know who puts a roof over your head? And feeds you at least three meals a day? And hugs you a million times a day and listens to you talk about your impossible inventions and your boring books and your absurd video games? The LEAST you could do is one measly chore!*

It's often then, as I really ramp up the indignation, that I feel a twinge in my spirit. In His gentle, loving way, God uses my kids' grumbling to remind me of all the times I've resisted His instruction or complained about my own responsibilities. *Oops*. And so, once again, I forgive my kids the way God forgives me, and together we get to work doing the things that need to be done. This time without grumbling or arguing!

Heavenly Father, thank You for being patient with me and for helping me grow in obedience and gratitude. I'm sorry for all the times I've resisted doing the work You've given me, grumbling about my own chores or responsibilities just like my kids do. Please give me the desire to follow You, even when it's not easy or convenient, and help me teach my kids to do the same. Amen.

God, show us the beauty

IN ALL OF YOUR CREATION,

INCLUDING THE BEAUTY

in ourselves.

Running Out of Gas

School spirit days: Causing meltdowns at my house since 2013. 😳

❄ 31 ❄

WHEN YOUR CHECK ENGINE LIGHT IS ON

Don't you realize that your body is the temple of the Holy
Spirit, who lives in you and was given to you by God? You
do not belong to yourself, for God bought you with a high
price. So you must honor God with your body.

1 Corinthians 6:19–20

Have you ever seen, or perhaps shared, a funny mom
meme that says "It's wine o'clock somewhere" or "Running errands is my cardio"? I have—more times than I care to
count! Parenting is hard, and adding ourselves to the list of
bodies we're caring for seems like too much to ask. For many
of us, the last thing we want to do when we get a few minutes
of down time is step on the treadmill or prep healthy snacks
for the week. In the moment, it feels much more comforting
and comfortable to veg on the couch, eat a few handfuls of
the chips we hide in the back of the pantry, or—my personal

favorite—stay up way too late because the quiet time is too lovely to resist.

As it turns out, though, God created our bodies as instruments for doing and enjoying the work He's given us. So while going to bed earlier, drinking more water, scheduling that annual exam, or adding fruits and veggies to our plate might not be fun, easy, or comfortable, it's worth it to know we're honoring God by taking good care of the body He gave us. And believe it or not, doing so will leave us refreshed and ready to jump back into our everyday life more than the most delicious doughnut or reality show ever will.

God, thank You for this body You gave me. I'm in awe of Your creativity and artistry, and I want to honor You by taking care of Your creation—including myself. It's hard, though, because I'm tired and stressed out, so I need Your help. Give me the determination I need to take baby steps toward a healthier body, as well as the compassion for myself when I fall short of my goals. Heal the parts of my body that are weary and hurting, and give me strength to choose the things that are truly good for my body. Amen.

⚛ 32 ⚛

WHEN YOU WONDER
WHAT WORK IS BEST

For we are God's masterpiece. He has created us anew in
Christ Jesus, so we can do the good things he planned
for us long ago.

Ephesians 2:10

Since having children, I've worked full-time, stayed home full-time, and managed at least a dozen variations of a part-time job (sometimes from home, sometimes not). No matter what my paycheck or planner looks like, though, I am always a working mom—and you are too. Whether or not you are employed outside your home, you work incredibly hard to provide for your family in one way or another. And no matter how straight or twisty, paved or primitive your career path has been, you were created with a purpose only you can fulfill.

As inspiring and encouraging as that thought may be, figuring out our purpose and how to fulfill it while also parenting can sometimes feel like just another task on an already overwhelming to-do list—and who needs that?! Thankfully, God is not only our creator but also our partner, guiding us as we uncover His plans for our lives at the office, at home, and everywhere in between. Deciding whether you should start a business, go back to school, work from home, or take the promotion? Take it to the Lord and let Him guide you to the next good thing He has planned for you.

Dear God, I'm not sure what to do. I believe that You made me for a reason and that You have a plan for me, but how do I know what it is? Will You show me? And no matter which path I choose, will You help me manage it alongside all the other things on my plate—like my marriage, kids, and home? It's so easy to feel like I have to do it all and do it perfectly, but I know that's not what You expect. Show me what matters most in each moment, Lord, and help me to honor You and the responsibilities You've given me in this season. Amen.

✺ 33 ✺

WHEN YOUR WORDS ARE MORE CRITICAL THAN CARING

You are altogether beautiful, my darling;
there is no flaw in you.

Song of Songs 4:7 NIV

Remember the story of David and Goliath? Before David went out to fight the giant, King Saul tried to prepare and protect him by putting his own heavy, oversized armor on David's slight frame. As he stumbled and his knees buckled under the weight, David realized he'd be better off without the armor, and as we know, he went on to victory with only a sling and a few stones.

Sometimes my parenting looks a little like that. I weigh down my kids with the armor I've built for myself over a lifetime. I tell myself and them that I'm preparing them to face the world, but really I'm hurting more than helping by placing my own fears and insecurities on their shoulders.

Critical by nature, I'm realizing that pointing out every error or attempting to quiet every quirk in an effort to protect my kids from the ridicule or disapproval of others isn't helpful. Rather than keeping them safe from self-doubt, I've created insecurity. I've done the exact thing I was trying to prevent! So while I still remind them to brush their hair and their teeth (it's basic hygiene!), I'm also working on seeing them—and speaking to them—the way God sees them: as beautiful and without flaw.

God, I don't know how You can look at me and call me beautiful or flawless. I feel just the opposite! And I realize now that I've been taking all my own insecurities and my fears that the world will be unkind and placing them on my kids. I've hurt them more than I've helped. Thank You, God, for opening my eyes to the truth. Help me change the way I talk to my kids. I don't want to unintentionally tear them down in an effort to perfect and protect them, and I don't want to flatter them with false compliments. Help me see and remember and speak over them the truth that they are wonderfully made, fully loved, and beautiful inside and out. Amen.

✺ 34 ✺

WHEN YOU FIND A PARTNER IN PARENTING

Two are better than one because they have a good reward for their efforts. For if either falls, his companion can lift him up; but pity the one who falls without another to lift him up. Also, if two lie down together, they can keep warm; but how can one person alone keep warm? And if someone overpowers one person, two can resist him. A cord of three strands is not easily broken.

Ecclesiastes 4:9–12 CSB

everal years ago one of my best friends stayed overnight at my home so we could drive together to a weekend retreat. Before we could hit the road, I had to get my kids out the door to school. That should have been a simple process, except that morning it was anything but simple. One of my daughters had a broken leg and, long story short, that made our lives enormously challenging for several months. On that particular morning she did not want to go to school and made her feelings abundantly clear. Later, as we finally began our trip, I wondered aloud if I could keep going and fighting this battle alone. My sweet friend reminded me that I wasn't alone. Then, instead of judging me for not keeping control of my kids or of my own emotions (which was what I'd feared she might do), she offered only understanding and assurance that the way I had handled the situation secured my status as supermom in her eyes.

I promise I'm no superhero, but I took that grace and held on tight. And when I experienced a frustratingly similar morning with that same child more recently, I didn't think twice before telling my friend all about it—including the way I'd lost my temper in a pretty ugly way. Once again, her words of understanding and encouragement demonstrated how well she knows and loves both me and my kids. As I heard her speak truth and love over me that morning, my jaw unclenched and my heart hurt a bit less. I thanked her for always being on my team—and I thanked God for giving me a partner in this hard business of parenting.

God, thank You for placing people in my life who support me as a mom and help bear the burden of raising these kids. Thank You for the ones partnering with me in the process, who keep me from losing my mind. You know I haven't always felt like I had someone to lean on, so I'm even more grateful to have someone now. As the kids grow and we do too, help us continue understanding, supporting, and encouraging each other. Help us be kind and respectful, even when we disagree about what's best for our kids. And please show us ways to lift one another up in our parenting journeys. Amen.

God, help me trust

YOU TO KEEP THE

WORLD TURNING,

EVEN WHEN I STOP TO REST.

❧ 35 ❧

WHEN YOU NEED TO PICK YOUR BATTLES

For the training of the body has limited benefit, but godliness is beneficial in every way, since it holds promise for the present life and also for the life to come.

1 Timothy 4:8 CSB

*J*ust eat the broccoli and quit complaining!"

"Don't forget to brush your teeth. And your hair!"

"You'd better clean up this mess before I come back up here."

I'm a pro at sweating the small stuff, at picking *every* battle— and using checklists and expectations that unintentionally drive a wedge between my children and me. When I was a new mom, I poured my energy into being the perfect parent and producing the perfect child, not realizing that every bit of that goal was impossible. Eventually I learned better, but it's still challenging to remember that the right words and actions aren't the end goal; instead, they're indications of our heart health. Just like God is more concerned about the state of our hearts than with how well we follow the rules or check the boxes, making our kids' emotional and spiritual health our priority will move our families so much closer to godliness than a clean bedroom ever could.

God, thank You for the privilege of parenting. Thank You for trusting me to teach my children about the things that matter most. Please help me focus on what's truly important and beneficial instead of getting lost in everything I want my child to do (or not do). Give me grace for them no matter how they behave and an affection for them that cannot be quenched by our everyday battles. And thank You for showing me affection that's everlasting and grace that's unending, even when my own behavior doesn't meet a single expectation or check a single box. Thank You for loving me. Help me share that love with my kids. Amen.

⚘ 36 ⚘

WHEN WORRY IS
YOUR FIRST REACTION

Therefore I tell you: Don't worry about your life, what you will eat or what you will drink; or about your body, what you will wear. Isn't life more than food and the body more than clothing? Consider the birds of the sky: They don't sow or reap or gather into barns, yet your heavenly Father feeds them. Aren't you worth more than they? Can any of you add one moment to his life span by worrying?

Matthew 6:25–27 CSB

My first instinct when faced with any dilemma is to worry about it. I might say I'm considering my options or making plans for handling it, but the truth is that I'm trying to control the situation by obsessing over every single angle or possibility. The truth is that I'm worrying. And while I'd gotten a little better about worrying less and trusting God more before I had kids, becoming a parent shifted my worries back into high gear.

Jesus said we shouldn't worry about anything—our lives, what we eat, what we wear. He didn't specifically include our children in that list, but I suspect He doesn't want us worrying about them either. And it makes sense when we read the rest of what He said. God cares for the birds and the flowers, so of course He's going to care for us. Knowing that, we can rest a little more easily. When we hear Jesus say that worrying doesn't accomplish anything, we can settle into a more peaceful posture and trust Him with our kids. It's not easy for any mom, but God will take care of our kids, and He will help us worry less.

Dear God, thank You for loving me—and my kids—so much. I know that if You care so well for the birds of the air and the flowers of the field, You'll certainly care for us too. But sometimes I forget. And sometimes I think that if I can just anticipate every single thing that could go wrong, I can keep any of it from happening. Please forgive me when I forget that I'm not in control. Help me remember the truth and trust in You more. Help me worry less, Lord. Amen.

⪘ 37 ⪗

WHEN PARENTING WEARS YOU DOWN

And let us not grow weary of doing good, for in due season we will reap, if we do not give up.

Galatians 6:9 ESV

've heard parenting older kids called "a different kind of exhausting." Now that my kids rarely wake up in the night, can make their own breakfast, and can usually pick out a clean-ish outfit to wear . . . I get it. Because while I don't have to change a dozen diapers or fix a dozen bottles each day, I do get to field dozens of questions (only some of which I know how to answer), break up dozens of arguments, and research dozens of song lyrics, movie references, social media apps, school electives, and summer camps. Add in discipline and consequences and attitudes and deep, philosophical questions about half an hour past bedtime, and yep, it's exhausting!

Another cup of coffee or a few rounds of deep breathing might seem like our best tool for surviving this stage, but what works even better is leaning into the patient, persevering love God has for us—and has given us for these kids. Only then will we make it through one more round of "Why do I have to take another shower?" and "Do you think superheroes believe in God?" and even "Let me tell you all the details of my video game again."

God, I'm so tired. My body is tired, yes, but even more so, my mind and my heart are exhausted. I'm not sure I can take another question, another debate, another argument, another dilemma to be solved. Some days I just want to give up. I'm worn out and worn down; I don't have anything left to offer them, Lord. Help me? Give me the strength and patience I need to keep going, to keep parenting, to keep doing the good work You have given me. Help me fix my eyes on the harvest so I can keep planting and nourishing today. Amen.

⁓ 38 ⁓

WHEN YOU'RE FALLING ASLEEP AT THE WHEEL

Come to me, all of you who are weary and burdened, and I will give you rest. Take up my yoke and learn from me, because I am lowly and humble in heart, and you will find rest for your souls. For my yoke is easy and my burden is light.

Matthew 11:28–30 CSB

If one thing is universal among moms, it's that we're all tired. No matter how many kids you have, no matter what kind of work you do, no matter where you live or what you look like or what kind of car you drive—if you're a mom, you're probably tired. But there's tired . . . and then there's exhausted, worn out, weary.

Tired is temporary. It's an inevitable side effect of raising little people into bigger people. Little people whose needs seem to be strongest in the wee hours of the early morning or late night. Tired is the obvious result of juggling work and home and family and personal responsibilities. But exhaustion sets in when we never get a break from all the things tiring us out. Weariness seeps into our soul the way tiredness penetrates our bones. And when we find ourselves in that exhausted, weary place, the only one big and soft and strong enough to ease that burden is God Himself. He can—and He will. We only need to ask.

God, I'm exhausted. So very weary. I feel like I'm constantly running, juggling, spinning until I'm dizzy—and then, after I fall down, I have to pick myself back up and start the same cycle. But I know You promise to give me rest; You tell me that You'll catch me when I fall and help me up once I've caught my breath. So God, I come to You today and ask You to catch me. Show me where I need to set some new boundaries, where I can push pause, and where I can take a break. Help me trust You to keep the world turning, even when I stop to rest. Thank You, Lord. Amen.

⚜ 39 ⚜

WHEN ANGER GETS THE BEST OF YOU

My dear brothers and sisters, take note of this: Everyone should be quick to listen, slow to speak and slow to become angry, because human anger does not produce the righteousness that God desires.

James 1:19–20 NIV

Recently I heard a friend say that she never yells at her kids, that she's just not much of a yeller. I wasn't sure how to respond, because unlike my friend, I yell at my kids all the time. I also regularly roll my eyes and frequently cry tears of frustration. And if slamming doors burned calories, I'd need to carbo-load every other day. It's 100 percent OK that we parent differently, and I know anger itself isn't a sin. But ever since that conversation, I've been thinking about how outbursts of anger usually produce more anger and strife long before any healthy resolution is reached.

Emotions aren't good or bad, and honestly expressing our feelings beats stuffing them down any day. So to my fellow moms who yell, don't think I'm saying that yelling makes you a bad mom. But I'm realizing that when we unleash our anger indiscriminately (and model that to our kids), it not only doesn't solve any problems but also leads us further from the life God wants for us. I might always have a temper, but these days I'm asking God to help me become less of a yeller and more of the mom He made me to be.

God, I'm sorry I yelled again. I'm sorry I was quick to become angry instead of being quick to listen to You and to my loved ones. Forgive me, Lord, and please help me grow in this area. When we face hard situations, help me be the one to model a calm spirit and find solutions instead of bringing more chaos and snap judgments. Give me patience and self-control, and protect me from the anger that threatens to overwhelm and derail me. Amen.

40

WHEN YOU NEED A FRIEND

A friend loves at all times,
and a brother is born for adversity.

Proverbs 17:17 ESV

One of my favorite former coworkers happens to live in the same small town I now call home. Though we celebrated our new proximity when my family moved here five years ago, I can count on one hand the number of times we've seen each other since then—and one of those times was a chance meeting at the grocery store. Making space and time for friends is hard for all of us moms, isn't it? Simply reaching out to someone can feel intimidating, and even when we muster the courage to send the text or walk across the street, our friendship problems aren't easily solved.

Everything from busy schedules to different parenting philosophies can keep us isolated from fellow moms, even though we've been hit over the head with reminders that "it takes a village." How do we find the mom friends we long for? How do we find the time to spend with them? How do we navigate the challenges of grown-up friendships? We start by asking God to help us, that's how. He intentionally created us to desire community and camaraderie, so when we ask Him for the courage and creativity to find friends or to make time for the ones we already have, He will help us.

God, I'm lonely. I miss the days of spending hours with a friend on the phone or at a coffee shop. That feels like a fairy tale now. But I don't need slumber parties or a weekly girls' night out. I'm just asking for someone who gets me, who gets my life, and who has a few minutes here and there to commiserate and encourage. Please send me a friend, God, and then give me the boldness to pursue her friendship and the commitment and compassion to maintain it. I know how important it is to spend time with those who lift me up and point me to You. Please send me that friend, God, and make me that friend for someone else. Amen.

God, help me fix my eyes

ON THE HARVEST

SO I CAN KEEP PLANTING

AND NOURISHING TODAY.

Shifting Gears and Changing Lanes

Me: Gets in the car to take 7yo to school, cranks up the radio when I hear an old favorite song.

7yo: "Mommy, what does 'diggity' mean?"

Me (unconcerned): "Ahh, I'm not sure."

Me (remembering the time I realized what the rest of the song's lyrics mean): Turns off the radio.

❧ 41 ❧

WHEN YOU FACE CHOICES
ABOUT SCHOOL

Cry out for insight,
    and ask for understanding.
Search for them as you would for silver;
    seek them like hidden treasures.
Then you will understand what it means to fear
      the LORD,
    and you will gain knowledge of God.

Proverbs 2:3–5

*P*arenting can feel like a never-ending pop quiz as we get peppered with questions we didn't even know to study for. And one question that comes up over and over again for twelve years or more feels like one of the most crucial: What to do about school? From the day we decide whether to send our little one to preschool, we are constantly forced to figure out the best way for our kids to learn.

Some of us have the choice of public school, private school, or home school. Others are deciding if after-school care is necessary or if our neighbor can watch our kids until we get home from work. And many of us are sitting in meetings or seeking counsel for challenges we didn't know to expect. Through it all, we try to balance what's best for our kids with what's possible for our families, and it can all feel like too much! But God promises to give us wisdom—with or without an advanced degree in education or child psychology. He will meet us right where we are for the family we have and the situation we're facing.

So when you find yourself spinning in confusion or overwhelmed by all the options, take a moment to breathe and ask God to guide you. He will give you the wisdom you need.

God, I don't know what to do. I'm grateful to have options, even if some of them feel uncomfortable or even impossible. But I'm confused about what's best and what's necessary versus what's optional. Will You help me? Guide me to the resources that can clarify everything for me; point me in the direction of what's best for our family and the plans You have for us. I know You love my kids even more than I do. Please show me what's right for them in this season. Amen.

✺ 42 ✺

WHEN THEY NEED FRIENDS

Carry each other's burdens, and in this way you will fulfill the law of Christ.

Galatians 6:2 NIV

'd like to believe that I will always have the soothing words, sage advice, hugs, or hot tea my children need when life is hard. I'd like to believe that as they grow, they'll turn to me every time they need help or comfort or guidance or strength. But I know that may not always be true. I know the day will likely come when either I'm not available or they truly need the perspective or support of someone their own age—someone who "gets it."

When that day comes, I'm praying my kids have a solid friend or two they can lean on. I'm praying they find "their people," the ones who understand and accept them but also point them toward good, healthy choices more often than not. We can't be our kids' only supporters forever, and they will need friends—especially as they grow older. Let's pray for those friends, and when they show up, let's welcome them into our family and trust them to stand with our kids through both good and hard times.

God, thank You for friendship and the strength and comfort it can bring. Please send my child a good friend or two, someone who will understand them and care about them and stand by them through the years. Especially when life becomes challenging or confusing, Lord, I ask that You will surround my kiddo with friends who provide unwavering support and wise counsel. Show them how to pursue healthy friendships, how to be a good friend to others, and how to nurture the friendships You give them. Amen.

☙ 43 ☙

WHEN YOUR KIDS GET HURT

Those who live in the shelter of the Most High
will find rest in the shadow of the Almighty.
This I declare about the LORD:
He alone is my refuge, my place of safety;
he is my God, and I trust him.

Psalm 91:1–2

We're calling an ambulance. Which hospital do you prefer?" That's not a call any mom wants to receive. Really, most of us could probably fill several bullet journals with a list of the calls we don't want to receive and the news we don't want to hear when it comes to all the ways our children's safety can be threatened. When I answered the phone that day and learned my daughter had broken her leg on a school field trip, I immediately began texting everyone—asking a friend to watch my youngest daughter, asking my mom to meet me at the hospital, asking my friends to pray. Only once I got in the car and started the longest twenty-minute drive of my life did I remember to actually pray myself.

But even though I was slow to turn to Him, the Lord was right there waiting to hold me close and to assure me that He was doing the same for my daughter. Of course I would rather that she never get hurt, but I'm grateful to remember that even while we face danger here on earth, we can find refuge in the Lord Most High. No matter how safe our children are (or aren't), God is with them. He alone can protect them, and He will.

God, please keep my children safe. Please hold them close and protect them from all the ways this broken world can hurt them. And when they do get hurt, which I know is inevitable, stay with them. Cover them with Your mercy and Your healing power. Keep them tethered to the truth of Your love and help them trust You in every circumstance. And please do that for me too: Keep me safe so I can care for them as long as they need me. Protect me and hold me close. Help me remember that You are with me no matter what. Amen.

❧ 44 ❧

WHEN YOU'RE THANKFUL FOR TEACHERS

Therefore, my dear brothers and sisters, stand firm. Let nothing move you. Always give yourselves fully to the work of the Lord, because you know that your labor in the Lord is not in vain.

1 Corinthians 15:58 NIV

Sometimes when I think about my children's teachers, I get so overwhelmed I could cry. Now, I might be more emotional than you, but I'm sure we can agree: the impact of the adults and authority figures in our kids' lives cannot be overstated. The coaches, instructors, counselors, and mentors they encounter over the years will reach them and influence them in ways parents can't always manage. (After all, which of us hasn't experienced the frustration of our child taking the same advice we gave them when it's offered by someone else?)

Anyone who instructs, invests in, and connects with young people faces enormous challenges and risks exhaustion and burnout. And while my gratitude for the kind, encouraging, gifted leaders in my kids' lives is boundless, most parents have learned the hard way that not all leaders are equipped for their roles. So while we pray for our kids as they go to school or practice or camp, let's also pray for those grown-ups who meet them there. Let's ask God to provide our kids with excellent adult influences outside our home, while also asking Him to encourage and strengthen the ones doing that work.

God, thank You for the adults making a difference in my child's life. And when I feel alone, please open my eyes to see and appreciate the other people on our team. I know how draining it can be to constantly reach out to and pour into kids, so I pray You don't let them become depleted. Please give them strength and support. Remind them of their sacred calling to influence young people, and show them the difference they're making. And help me be a support to them, showing them grace and gratitude through my words and actions. Amen.

45

WHEN THEY ARE DETERMINED TO BE UNIQUE

> But our bodies have many parts, and God has put each part just where he wants it. How strange a body would be if it had only one part! Yes, there are many parts, but only one body.
>
> 1 Corinthians 12:18–20

Are you sure you don't want to try soccer again?" I've asked my youngest daughter that at least half a dozen times. And every time she politely (though insistently) says no thanks. We signed her up for soccer a couple years ago, when her two best friends were also playing—but unlike her friends, she didn't fall in love with the sport. She loves reading books about soccer, and one of her favorite TV shows is about a girl who plays soccer. But doing it herself? *No thanks.*

Neither of my kids has shown a lasting interest in most of the things I love. They are persistently (and unapologetically) their own unique selves. And I'm so grateful for that! Though it has taken me a while to get past my expectations of who they would be, I'm thankful that God has created them to be different from me, different from each other, and different from their friends. How boring life would be if we were all the same!

Do you struggle with allowing your kids to be fully themselves? Remember that those quirks and their unusual talents or interests are all part of God's intentional masterpiece, lovingly placed in our children for a purpose.

God, thank You for making my kids the way You did! They are not who or what I expected, but I know that's not only OK but also a blessing. I know every part of them—their interests, their inclinations, the inventive ways they look at the world—is Your magnificent design, and I love all of those parts. Help me remember that, Lord, when I struggle with the ways they're different from me or from their peers. Help me love them well. Amen.

❧ 46 ❧

WHEN YOU NEED TO REMEMBER GOD IS ALWAYS WITH YOU (AND YOUR KIDS)

The LORD is with me; I will not be afraid.
What can mere mortals do to me?

Psalm 118:6 NIV

I sat in the middle school cafeteria, awkwardly balancing my adult body on the hard, skinny bench made for kids. Even more awkward? The tears threatening to spill down my cheeks and the hitch in my breath. I was at the school for an informational meeting about an upcoming student trip, and I was surprised by the fear that suddenly gripped me. I expected to feel excited and nostalgic as I learned about the possibility of my daughter taking the same cross-country trip I'd taken in the eighth grade. Instead, I was panicking at the thought of letting her board an airplane and travel to our nation's capital without me.

Later, when I got home and skimmed the travel brochure, I realized that part of my unexpected reaction was understandable in light of a simple timeline. I had traveled without my parents on a school trip to Washington, DC, several years before the events of 9/11. While I'm sure my parents had worried, I recognized that sending my daughter on this same trip brought up different concerns for me than it did for them. And yet, I still wanted my daughter to have this experience, so I knew I had to lay all my (quite reasonable) fears at God's feet.

Am I saying my hand didn't shake when I clicked "submit" on the sign-up form? Nope. Or that my breath hasn't caught and my voice hasn't faltered when my daughter and I discuss payment plans or possible roommates? No way. And when it comes time to drop her at the airport, I don't expect to drive home without a single tear (more likely it will be a whole bucketful). But I'm choosing to trust God with my kid—no matter how near or far she is from me, she's never out of His reach.

Thank You, God, for being with me and with my kids. Thank You for promising to never leave us and to always protect us. I trust You with my children and place them confidently in Your hands because I know You love them even more than I do. I trust You to protect them, to guide them, to show them the way to go as they take steps into the world (and away from me). Help me trust You even more so I can be an example for my kids to do the same. Remind them that You are always with them and they don't have to be afraid. Give us courage as we trust You every day. Amen.

✺ 47 ✺

WHEN THEY'RE CHOOSING MENTORS

Remember your leaders who have spoken God's word to you. As you carefully observe the outcome of their lives, imitate their faith.

Hebrews 13:7 CSB

Both my kids grow attached to people very quickly. They've been crushed when friends move away, and saying good-bye to their teachers brings tears every year. I have to admit they come by this tendency honestly—I'm still Facebook friends with my middle school music teacher and a best friend who moved across the country when I was ten years old. It's endearing and understandable (at least to me), but it's also risky. Becoming attached to and fond of someone so quickly and so deeply often means that person has great influence on you.

When I think of my own childhood and consider whose influence I feel to this day, I remember some adults who encouraged me and taught me what it looks like to follow God—and others who decidedly did not. My prayer for my kids today is that they'll encounter more of the former than the latter, that they'll be protected from unhealthy influences and pointed toward those adults who will love them and lead them well. I'm praying for those mentors to show up, to persevere in teaching and leading by example, and to be blessed for their generosity and faithfulness.

Dear God, thank You for the mentors and teachers who were excellent examples and helped me grow in my faith. Please give my children that same gift of having other adults in their lives who will care about them deeply and will commit to mentoring them even if just for a season. Open our eyes to those people so we don't miss them! And give them wisdom as they teach my kids. Give them strength to faithfully follow You so they live lives worth imitating. Protect my kids from unhealthy or harmful influences; point them toward mentors who will show them Your goodness and love. Thank You, God. Amen.

✵ 48 ✵

WHEN YOU THINK ABOUT THE FUTURE

Many are the plans in the mind of a man,
but it is the purpose of the LORD that will stand.

Proverbs 19:21 ESV

What do you want to be when you grow up?"

Why do we insist on asking kids this question? Do we really expect them to know their dream job at nine years old? Some days I still don't know what I want to be when I grow up! But for whatever reason, this is a go-to question we ask kids of all ages. My second-grader wants to be a basketball player and a scientist who studies rocks (perhaps to justify her ever-growing rock collection). On the other hand, my daughter in middle school has begun to realize just how many career options there are and tends to answer this question with sputtering exclamations of how she *just! doesn't! know!*

I remind them (and myself) that fortunately we don't have to decide yet. Not only that, but I remind them (and myself) that it's OK if they change their mind and end up choosing a different path. After all, we know from Scripture that God has a purpose for them that He will make clear and accessible in His perfect timing. No matter if they become scientists or artists or entrepreneurs or plumbers, they will be part of God's grand plan. And that will never change.

God, thank You for having good plans for each and every one of us. You know how much I'd like to plan out my kids' lives, but I trust that Your purpose for them (and for me) is something better than I could even imagine. As my kids make plans for their lives, please help them hold those dreams loosely and pursue wisdom and guidance from You with every step. Lord, help me do the same, following Your plans with bold faith as an example for them. Help me trust You with their lives and with mine. Amen.

❧ 49 ❧

WHEN YOU NEED TO TAKE
YOUR HANDS OFF THE WHEEL

You, my brothers and sisters, were called to be free. But do
not use your freedom to indulge the flesh; rather, serve one
another humbly in love. For the entire law is fulfilled in keeping this one command: "Love your neighbor as yourself."

Galatians 5:13–14 NIV

The summer my oldest daughter decided to save up her
money so she could make a couple large purchases on
her own was challenging. Not because she had few opportunities to earn money and became a little obsessed with all
things financial (though that concerned me too!). The challenge was in allowing her room to grow in responsibility and
independence. In other words, I had to bite my tongue when
she decided to spend her precious earnings on candy or stick-
ers, even though her next babysitting gig wasn't scheduled
for three more weeks.

When we are given guidance or correction, something inside most of us—kids and adults alike—makes us resist authority and yearn to shout, "You're not the boss of me!" As our kids grow up and are given more choices and responsibilities, they often feel giddy with power and freedom. That's when it becomes our job to coach them how to use their freedom well—in healthy ways that honor God and help others—while also prying our hands off their proverbial steering wheels. It can be so hard (so! hard!), but our heavenly Father knows a thing or two about allowing His children to make their own choices, and He will guide us.

God, thank You for the ways my kids are growing up. They're so amazing—smart and kind and talented and loving. But they're also still kids. And just like I am still making mistakes as I learn, they are bound to mess up. I don't want them to be hurt by poor choices, Lord. I don't want them to suffer or struggle, and sometimes I wish I could dictate their every move for the rest of their lives. OK, that's not completely true—I want to watch them grow and learn and fly. Help me coach them through this next stage as they test their wings. Help me continue to teach them when they will listen and to hold my tongue when they need my silent support. Help me always be a soft place for them to land, just like You are for me. Amen.

☙ 50 ☙

WHEN IT'S TIME TO BEGIN LETTING GO

For everything there is a season,
     a time for every activity under heaven.
A time to be born and a time to die.
     A time to plant and a time to harvest. . . .
A time to cry and a time to laugh.
     A time to grieve and a time to dance.

Ecclesiastes 3:1–2, 4

The other day I took my daughter to the pool to go swimming with her friend. After chatting with her friend's mom for a few minutes, I turned to leave. "Bye!" I called to my daughter. "I'll be back in an hour or so." My girl barely glanced my way and certainly didn't run back to give me a hug. Which makes sense—she's thirteen years old. But for a moment, all I could see (other than the back of her head as she resumed her very important conversation) was her much younger self sobbing when I dropped her off at daycare, then preschool, and even kindergarten.

She's not that girl anymore. And that's a good thing! Our goal, after all, is to raise our babies into strong, independent adults who leave our homes and live on their own. Right? *Right*. Our kids are going to grow up. They're doing it even now (whether we like it or not)! God is here to help us through every change, every ending, every goodbye as our kids do exactly what they're supposed to do and grow up.

God, thank You for all the ways my kids are learning and growing. It's incredible watching them turn into their own people, confident and curious about everything the world offers. But, as You know, it's also hard to watch them grow up! It's hard watching them go to school, to camp, to a new job or on a first date—even though I'm so proud of them. I miss them already, and they aren't even gone yet. But I know they'll go eventually; they'll start their own lives and take my heart with them. Help me, Lord? Give me courage as I begin letting go, give me wisdom as I learn how to parent in each new stage, and help me trust You completely. Amen.

God, help me always be

A SOFT PLACE FOR

MY KIDS TO LAND,

just like You are for me.

A Final Note

Well, friend, we've made it to the end (although we all know that mom life never really ends). Whether you skipped around finding what worked for you in the moment or worked through the entries from first to last, I hope you've found a little more peace than you had before you opened *Prayers from the Parking Lot*.

As you may have noticed as I shared some stories with you, I do not have this all figured out. And for our purposes here, "this" could mean parenting, walking in faith, trusting God with what (or who) I value most in the world—or all of the above! This thing we're doing is hard, and on any given day I'm as likely as anyone to be stressed out or feel clueless. I promise.

But that's why I wrote this book—for you and for me. That's why it's imperative that we keep turning back to God over and over, every time we feel the panic rise up, every time we feel the weight of doubt and fear and even shame. It's why God invites us into His presence whenever and wherever we steal a moment to close our eyes and breathe—in the bathroom, in the closet, or in the car as we sit in the parking lot for just a minute longer.

Whether we're reading a prayer someone else wrote, whispering the most personal, vulnerable words we can't even believe we're saying out loud, or simply letting loose the tears, the sighs, or the screams of frustration we've been holding back—every single time we turn to God, He meets us there.

So today, as you reach for the door handle and prepare to face your people, your life, your challenges once again, may you feel His presence go with you. May you move forward in the wisdom and strength He's offering you, remembering that He has created you for this moment and will give you everything you need. May you be filled with the joy of the Lord until you once again find time to pray in the parking lot.

MARY CARVER writes and speaks with humor and honesty, encouraging women with truth found in unexpected places. She is a regular contributor to (in)courage, the author of *Women of Courage, Journey to the Cross,* and the (in)courage Bible studies *Courageous Joy* and *Create in Me a Heart of Hope,* as well as the coauthor of *Choose Joy, Sacred Tears,* and *Empowered.* Mary lives in Kansas City with her husband and two daughters. Find her online at www.marycarver.com.

Connect with
MARY

Follow Mary online, visit her website **MaryCarver.com**, and for more encouragement, be sure to follow her podcast, *The Couch*, wherever podcasts are found.

Follow Mary on social media

 @Marycarver    Mary Carver

COME AS YOU ARE—FOR REAL—
and know that God cares about
every aspect of your life

Read more of Mary's writing in *Empowered*, an (in)courage devotional designed to help you cultivate each area of your life to live fully as God created you to be. Through Scripture, stories, prayers, and reflection questions, you will learn to stop compartmentalizing your faith, reject the lie that you're not worthy, and live each day in the truth of God's Word.